7 PRAYERS
for Discernment and Decision-Making

A Group Prayer Process to Find God's Direction

KIM BUTTS

PRAYERSHOP
PUBLISHING

Terre Haute, Indiana

PrayerShop Publishing is the publishing arm of the Church Prayer Leaders Network. The Church Prayer Leaders Network exists to equip and inspire local churches and their prayer leaders in their desire to disciple their people in prayer and to become a "house of prayer for all nations." Its online store, prayershop.org, has more than 150 prayer resources available for purchase or download.

ISBN (Print): 978-1-935012-86-3
ISBN: (E-Book): 978-1-935012-87-0

Scripture quotations marked (NIV) are taken from the Holy Bible, New International Version®, NIV®. Copyright © 1973, 1978, 1984, 2011 by Biblica, Inc.™ Used by permission of Zondervan. All rights reserved worldwide. www.zondervan.com The "NIV" and "New International Version" are trademarks registered in the United States Patent and Trademark Office by Biblica, Inc.™

Scripture quotations marked (NASB) are taken from the New American Standard Bible® (NASB), Copyright © 1960, 1962, 1963, 1968, 1971, 1972, 1973, 1975, 1977, 1995 by The Lockman Foundation. Used by permission. www.Lockman.org

Scripture quotations marked (MSG) are taken from THE MESSAGE, copyright © 1993, 2002, 2018 by Eugene H. Peterson. Used by permission of NavPress. All rights reserved. Represented by Tyndale House Publishers, Inc.

Scripture quotations marked (NLT) are taken from the Holy Bible, New Living Translation, copyright ©1996, 2004, 2015 by Tyndale House Foundation. Used by permission of Tyndale House Publishers, Inc., Carol Stream, Illinois 60188. All rights reserved.

1 2 3 4 5 | 2023 2022 2021 2020 2019

Acknowledgments

Thank you to my husband, Dave, for continually encouraging me to develop and finish this project! I will always be grateful for listening to God together as we seek to point leaders and churches toward becoming houses of prayer for all nations! Dave, your affirmation means so much!

My deep appreciation to Gary Black, senior pastor of Clayton Christian Church in Clayton, Indiana, for so generously giving of his time to carefully read through this manuscript. His thoughtful and valuable feedback greatly improved the material for leaders.

I'm also very grateful to Dr. John Caldwell, president of John Caldwell Ministries, retired senior pastor of Kingsway Christian Church in Avon, Indiana, and author of *Intimacy with God*. John also read through the manuscript and gave me affirmation and encouragement to keep moving forward with the project.

Thanks also to editor and publisher, Jonathan Graf, who is so good at keeping the intent of my content while shortening my "Apostle Paul" length sentences!

Table of Contents

Introduction   7

The Process   13

Steps of the Process   15

Suggestions to Strengthen and Shape the Process   25

7 Prayers for Discernment and Decision-Making   31

Moving Forward with Confidence   49

Extra Notes   55

Participant's Guide   57

7 Prayers for Discernment and Decision-Making   65
    (Participant's Guide)

Introduction

If you are on a leadership team, you know that getting a room full of leaders to come into agreement on any decision, even small ones, is often fraught with disagreement and differing opinions. That is unless the guidance of the Holy Spirit is brought into your corporate dynamic.

Inviting God into the process of decision-making should not be just an obligatory exercise because you are all believers and/or functioning in a Christian environment. Seeking His involvement as you discern a plan, or attempt to make the best possible decision (perhaps involving hiring a staff person or determining how best to spend funds), can bring everything into alignment with God's kingdom plans and purposes.

The full-blown process presented in this prayer tool is time-consuming. (I recommend a minimum of a two-day retreat setting for a major issue.) You will find, however, that the hours you spend to come to the right corporate decision, or to discern a major shift in operations, activity or location, will be time well spent. Why? Because your decision/discernment will not be based upon your own ideas, plans, egos, wisdom, etc., but upon the perfect will of God through the power of the Holy Spirit working in your midst. Would you rather have a "group think" decision or God's best plan as His Spirit reveals it to you within a season of corporate prayer and unity?

This process of discernment prayer can be helpful not only in corporate church, business, ministry, etc. settings, but is also adaptable for individuals, married couples and families. Additionally, this process may be employed by missionaries and missions organizations, small groups, ministry teams within a church, or in a situation where multiple churches or groups of churches from a variety of denominational backgrounds are planning an event together or looking to work together in unity for the purposes of God.

This discernment prayer format was originally developed in conjunction with what my ministry, Harvest Prayer Ministries, had developed as a tool to assist churches toward becoming a house of prayer for all nations (Isaiah 56:7 and Mark 11:17). We call this tool **Roadmap to a Praying Church.**

It is one thing to be convinced that prayer should be the foundational strategy for every aspect of church/business life and ministry. We don't find too many who don't believe this is the case after a profoundly impactful session on the theology of prayer. But what does a praying church look like and how does a church leadership move toward this goal? Being convinced is not the hard part for leaders and staff. *Discerning how to get there* is where the breakdown usually occurs. There are as many opinions about what a house of prayer should look like in a particular church culture as there are people making the decision. That's why we needed to develop this process.

Does this sound similar to some of the meetings you lead or attend where discernment and/or decision-making takes place?

Smaller, less-complicated decisions won't need to go through the full-blown process outlined in this guide. However, the principles and prayers can still be effectively applied and utilized. Every situation and context will be different just by nature of the type of decision/discernment to be made, and the composition of individuals involved. Anyone taking the main leadership role for guiding a team through the journey of discernment/decision-making, should give this guide a thorough read and glean what is most useful.

For major decisions or discernment, I suggest following this guide very closely in order to know that you have done your "due diligence" with God. Our time on earth is but a breath, so making wrong decisions or moves can not only slow us down, but cause great damage. If our processes are Spirit-led rather than subject to "group think" or the "democratic process" the outcomes will be significantly more kingdom focused, wise and fruitful.

A retreat setting often works best. Getting leaders away from the familiar and into a context where God can be sought apart from distractions such as cell phones, is a powerful dynamic.

Whether a major decision or a smaller issue that requires careful discernment, the key is coming to a consensus that is God-directed. This can only take place if the entire process is prayerfully God-focused, with each person being willing to submit what he or she "thinks" is the best way, to accept what God's agenda might be instead.

As an example, I will highlight one leadership team our ministry has worked with recently. These folks were a small group of prayer team members who had been diligently praying for their staff and church leadership to embrace Jesus' mandate from Mark 11:17 to become a house of prayer. They had become discouraged and seemed unable to come to a consensus as to how they should move forward as a team because their senior leadership didn't seem to be fully engaged in becoming a house of prayer for all nations.

I met with them in a retreat setting to pray together. They needed to discern how God might be leading them to function as a team given the situation they faced. They had been set apart by leadership for the task of prayer ministry for the church, but they knew that without full participation by elders, staff and other church leaders, their "ultimate goals" would go unmet in the present.

After a season of prayer, laying out their concerns and desires to see God move powerfully in their church leadership and congregation, to a person, they emerged with a fresh resolve that their "job" was not to criticize their leaders, but to pray more earnestly for them. They were not to complain, but to move forward within the parameters available to them and entrusted to them by church leaders.

They didn't take a vote, but instead, were brought into spiritual agreement through the power of God moving in and through them by the Holy Spirit. A huge burden was lifted off of this team of prayer leaders. They were ready to move forward to see what God might have for them to be and do rather than be stymied by the red tape they perceived stood in their way.

At this point, I gave them each a piece of paper and had them respond to this question: "What would a house of prayer for all nations look like within the culture of your faith community?" They were not to speak to one another or look at what anyone else was writing.

When they were all finished, I had them read what they had written one by one. As you might expect, there were some similarities; however, to a great extent their responses were all over the map. They were able to clearly see that there was a disparity in what they thought a house of prayer should look like at this point. They came to realize that much work lay ahead to determine how to come into a united consensus in order to move forward with some kind of plan.

When I do this particular exercise with the kind of church staff and leadership that *does* get the importance of being a house of prayer I then suggest they engage with the document you are looking at now. (You may assume that this applies to whatever leadership team you may be involved with that "gets" the big picture need for wise decision-making and/or discernment.)

Back to our small group of prayer leaders. After they were all in agreement to move forward with a fresh vision for what could be done with the prayer movement in their congregation, they were ready to answer a question. "If each of you has a different idea of what a house of prayer looks like (referring to the exercise they just completed on paper), how are you all going to work together to come into agreement about how to most effectively get there?"

They looked at me with that "deer in the headlights" kind of stare. "We don't know" was the response. "Pray?" Yep! Right answer. However, they couldn't even agree what to pray about.

At the time, *7 Prayers for Discernment and Decision-Making* was not yet completed. I did introduce several of the prayers that are in this resource as a way they might begin to seek God together. I led them through each, slowly. At the end of our retreat, this team had discerned a strong plan together. They were in full agreement with one another and were excited to implement what God had shown them. They also knew they could use these prayers whenever they felt "stuck" in their direction or decision-making. They had a tool to use that would lead them into the presence of God together, seeking His guidance for their ministry. These leaders now felt empowered and knew that *their* plan was really God's plan.

One thing to always keep in the forefront of your minds is this: Never assume that because the process looks difficult it must not be God's will. Sometimes that's exactly what it is because God has not chosen the easy road for the journey that lies ahead. Always consider that the ways of God through the working of His Spirit are not our own. He may have things to teach and some transformational truths to reveal, so don't short circuit this process when the going slows or the way is not smooth.

He is at work because you are asking Him to be. Matthew 18:20 says, "For where two or three have gathered together in My name, I am there in their midst" (NASB).

Whatever leadership context you are in—business, education,

church, missions, organization, etc.—you should be able to utilize and apply the prayers and processes found in this discernment and decision-making guide. My prayer is that it will align you and your team members with the plans and purposes of the kingdom of God.

—Kim Butts

The Process

The purpose of this guide is to provide a step by step process for discerning and implementing God's intent and desire as you seek His kingdom plan and purpose toward a specific goal, decision, need or solution. The process will include a season of preparation followed by the use of seven specific prayers to guide you into Spirit-led discernment and decision-making.

Important Notes:

- The team leader (selected through a process defined below) should work through this guide on his or her own prior to beginning the corporate discernment process with a team. This is very important and will allow the corporate group to move smoothly through to God's best conclusion. The person reading this material for the first time may not be the actual team leader, but the person who brings the need for this process to the attention of others.
- Feel free to recognize that there are several different ways this information can be implemented and applied. Utilize what

works best in your particular situation as you feel directed by the Holy Spirit.

Scripture instructs us to pray for discernment as we make decisions:

"For if you cry for discernment,
Lift your voice for understanding;
If you seek her as silver
And search for her as for hidden treasures;
Then you will discern the fear of the LORD
And discover the knowledge of God." *(Proverbs 2:3-5 NASB)*

"The Spirit searches all things, even the deep things of God. For who knows a person's thoughts except their own spirit within them? In the same way no one knows the thoughts of God except the Spirit of God. What we have received is not the spirit of the world, but the Spirit who is from God, sothat we may understand what God has freely given us. This is what we speak, not in words taught us by human wisdom but in words taught by the Spirit, explaining spiritual realities with Spirit-taught words. The person without the Spirit does not accept the things that come from the Spirit of God but considers them foolishness, and cannot understand them because they are discerned only through the Spirit. The person with the Spirit makes judgments about all things, but such a person is not subject to merely human judgments, for, 'Who has known the mind of the Lord so as to instruct him?' But we have the mind of Christ." *(1 Corinthians 2:10-16 NIV)*

Steps of the Process

Every church or ministry faces difficult decisions and times when it is vital to have good discernment in knowing what comes next, or how to proceed on a significant matter. Whenever a leadership team or board of directors is gathered, there is always the potential for division, disagreement and discouragement to creep into a process designed for seeking the way forward.

James reveals to us, God's people are susceptible to the sin of arrogant self-reliance when making "our" plans as opposed to aligning ourselves with His kingdom plans and purposes:

> "Look here, you who say, 'Today or tomorrow we are going to a certain town and will stay there a year. We will do business there and make a profit.' How do you know what your life will be like tomorrow? Your life is like the morning fog—it's here a little while, then it's gone. What you ought to say is, "If the Lord wants us to, we will live and do this or that." Otherwise you are boasting about your own pretentious plans, and all such boasting is evil. Remember, it is sin to know what you ought to do and then not do it." *(James 4:13-17 NLT)*

Scripture shows us a powerful plan by which God's people can move forward in decision-making to discern God's way, rather than struggle within our own limited understanding to make our own "pretentious plans." The discernment process outlined below will be centered around and shaped by seven scriptural prayers to help corporate teams come into agreement and alignment.

As followers of Christ, with the mind of Christ, it is crucial to seek the presence of God together so that His agenda, answers, plans and purposes can become our own. Often, we seem to have the audacity to ask God to bless what we are planning, have already planned, or what we have decided and discerned apart from Him. Instead, we should focus ourselves upon what God Himself directs us to that is aligned with His perfect will and purposes. God's glory should be our ultimate corporate goal and we should be resolved to settle for nothing less.

This spiritual process of discernment/decision-making is not a democracy.

There should be no voting, only united consensus. It is both an individual and corporate process. And clearly, as evidenced by 1 Corinthians 2: 10-16, discernment is tied to the Holy Spirit!

Conviction and sometimes conversion to another point of view will likely happen as the Spirit is invited into your process. When compromise becomes not a "settling" for something less, but a realization that this may be the direction God is leading in, it becomes a positive positional shift—cooperation instead of concession.

As you seek His perfect will in your decision-making process, God becomes the Revealer of His plan and purpose for your discernment rather than the "Blesser" of your own good ideas and plans. His way becomes the attractive and best choice (Your will be done on earth as it is in heaven). God will not force you to step into His will. He wants you to discover His best purposes and come alongside Him.

Although this process seems time-consuming you will find that you actually save much valuable time and have God's best outcome by seeking His perspective. If you will be open to discovering and then aligning yourselves with God's best decision/leading you will avoid unhealthy adversity and potential damage to relationships on your leadership team.

Note: Recognizing that the bylaws of your church, organization or school may require a vote regarding the issue you are focused upon, consider that after a season of discernment and/or decision-making you will likely have reached a 100% consensus. Voting may then take place as a formality to satisfy the requirements of your bylaws.

Essentials

"Seek the Kingdom of God above all else, and live righteously, and he will give you everything you need." *(Matthew 6:33 NLT)*

Step 1—Define the Issue:

Before beginning this prayer journey, it is important to clearly articulate for yourselves and to God what you are actually seeking His help with. For example, a church may sense that God's desire is for them to become a house of prayer for all nations (Isaiah 56:7, Mark 11:17), but they do not know how to begin or go about moving forward toward this end. Other needs may be: discerning the way forward when the way is as yet unknown or is unclear, choosing a new staff person, beginning a new business venture, etc.

As you formulate your focus, the most vital components to your issue are these questions:

- Is what we are seeking to accomplish, decide or discern something that comes from our own hearts or from the heart of God?
- Are we prepared for the possibility that God may change "our" plans and/or our trajectory?
- Ask Him for clarity so that what you are discerning or the decision you are making comes clearly from His heart and is not generated from your own needs or good ideas.

Note: Defining the issue will need to be revisited once the team is determined and a leader is identified. Keep referring back to James 4:13-17. Remind yourselves that your lives, and indeed, your decisions and plans, are but a mist unless they have kingdom impact beyond your own limited scope of thinking and desiring.

Step 2—Identify the Leadership:

It is imperative that everyone involved in making decisions or seeking discernment for your church, ministry, business, school or other organization is part of this process. All influencers must be engaged in this corporate process. If not, they should understand that they will not have a say in the implementation or actions that come out of this season. An entire team must have complete "buy-in" for this process to be fully God-directed. If someone is unable to participate in any season or session, the process should be delayed or changed so that everyone can be present. Using technology to connect with a team member is acceptable, but not optimal.

This process is not short and it is not easy. Every team member must be willing to be fully engaged.

Note: It is possible that the decision or the discernment that is needed, may be considered to be more at a micro level and may only be applicable to one area of the church or organization (for example, a certain department or ministry team). If so, and the leadership within this area is clearly delineated (including whatever supervisor or elder/deacon/pastor with oversight is included), this prayer process can be successfully engaged.

Step 3—Select a Team Leader:

An individual to lead the actual process needs to be chosen. The Leader, whose purpose is to shepherd the prayer process as directed by God, does not have to be the Lead Pastor, CEO or Board Chairperson. If the issue in question is one where a neutral person should be asked to take an impartial leadership role, it is vital to find someone who can guide the process objectively and in an unbiased way. Either way, the Leader must be someone who:

- acknowledges that the Director of the discernment process is God alone.
- is recognized by all participants of the process as spiritually prepared to take on such a vital leadership position.
- is known to be Spirit-led in his or her prayer life and has the confidence of the team to direct prayer times in this posture and attitude.
- is well-respected by all of the team members.
- understands that prayer is the strategy for being what God desires and for all of God's kingdom work.
- is able to guide others wisely, impartially and with great love.
- is willing to invest the time to be personally prepared and will adequately prepare the team.
- is patient with the process and willing to follow God's timetable rather than succumb to the temptation to bring things to a more rapid conclusion. He or she should be someone who is able to discern when it may be time to lay the process aside for a season

if the team is in need of reflection, redirection, or rest.

Specifics for the Team Leader:

1. Spiritual preparation is vital. As the Leader you should personally go through the **Prayers of Preparation** (pages 26-30) ahead of the group process. This will enable you to be able to encourage the rest of your team to do so prior to beginning your time of discernment prayer.

2. Be sure all of the details for the discernment retreat or meeting are initialized and finalized. It is optimal to find a place to engage this process that is away from church/business, etc. and where team members can be fully present to God. See specifics about location on page 23.

   Give all participants a list of what they will need to bring with them: Bibles, journals (if using them), etc. Each person should also have the **Participant version** of the Discernment Process. This is found on pages 57-77.

3. Take some time to initially familiarize yourself with the **7 Prayers of Discernment and Decision-Making** (Located on pages 31-48). Seek insight as to how God may wish to move in the midst of your team's discernment process. You will want to know the prayers well, so that, with the help of the Holy Spirit, you are best able to guide the team through this season of prayer. Determine if you or others will read through the content aloud, and otherwise shepherd how your team engages God within each season of prayer.

4. As Leader, you will guide not only the prayer process but also the discussion. Be careful not to micro-manage. Let the process move into and out of prayer naturally as the Spirit leads you. The times

for discussion, prayer, silence, worship, breaks, etc. will be clarified as you give Him control. Listen carefully to the Lord and to the team members during prayer and discussion/conversation.

If you sense that God is leading in a particular way, or that it is time to move to a different posture or season of prayer, guide the group in that direction. A caution should be considered here. P Douglas Small, in his book *The Praying Church Made Simple*, asserts that when engaging a group in corporate prayer, it is important not to fling out the "default" words, "everyone pray as the Spirit leads."

> "This is an amazing assumption, that all present are directed by the Holy Spirit; that all discern correctly and are not only perceptive enough to hear, but empowered to obey. No one should assume such a thing. We are too often influenced by personal agendas, by the sights and sounds of the imploding world around us, driven by fears more than faith."

He goes on to emphasize that when trying to discern the will and leading of God in a corporate setting that the time or season of prayer should be guided by someone who has yielded themselves to a Spirit-led posture. This leader should be able to escort others into the transformative presence of God for His kingdom purposes.

5. Stopping periodically to ask clarifying questions is valuable:

"What are you hearing from God?"
"Do you sense we are in agreement about this?"
"I believe we are moving in a new direction at this point. What do you think?"

It is also good to reiterate what has been shared from time to time:
"I hear (name of person) saying that…"
"It seems we are all feeling that the best strategy is to…"

Flowing from prayer to discussion and back into prayer is a fluid process. Allow and encourage others to share what they hear or sense from the Spirit along the way. Remind the team to be sensitive to one another without being judgmental. This process belongs to all of you, and the Holy Spirit can work through different people and ideas at different times as you create space for His Presence.

6. If and when you recognize that the enemy is attempting to stir up disunity, division, deception, discouragement, or doubt (see *The Devil Goes to Church* by David Butts), the team should be made aware of it immediately and the intercessors should be informed (see Step 4: Enlist Intercessors).

7. If a roadblock such as the one listed in #6 occurs while the group is meeting together, the leader should spend time with each person individually to determine if there is something or someone hindering the process. Notify the prayer team if there is a crucial need for a breakthrough so that they can press in on behalf of the team.

8. Determine when the process is successfully completed or if more time is needed. If unity has been accomplished, likely, the entire team will all know together when the moment of completion arrives. Lead the group in prayers of thanksgiving and worship.

9. If more time is needed than what has been allocated, schedule another time/season for prayer and continue.

Step 4—Enlist Intercessors:

It is a good idea and a valuable practice to have a team of intercessors who pray for and through the process. Before your corporate season of prayer takes place, gather a small, trusted group of people who will, with great care, bring this process and each participant before the throne of grace in the days prior to and during the journey of discovering God's plans and purposes. Personally invite each person rather than give a blanket invitation to "anyone who wants to" pray. Don't delegate this task to your church prayer team to save time. Query each team member for names of people they feel would be trustworthy and faithful intercessors.

The intercessors do not need every detail, but should be updated regularly and as need arises. If the team is "stuck" or facing spiritual warfare (for example: experiencing a threat of division or discouragement) and unable to move forward, the leader may choose to connect with the intercessors to ask them to press in for a breakthrough. One person on your leadership team and one person on the intercessory team should be in communication between the two groups.

If the intercessors hear from God on your behalf, they should connect with the team through the liaisons. Perhaps God has an entirely different direction for you prayerfully to consider together as revealed to you by those lifting up your process.

Step 5—Determine Location and Time Frame for the Process:

A corporate retreat setting is preferable with several hours, a full day or even an overnight two-day meeting devoted to this prayer journey. The time needed is directly proportional to the difficulty of the task before you. If you sense there is some initial disagreement or multiple choices that could be made, then time will be needed.

Because your team is likely made up of several individuals who all may have different ideas prior to engaging the prayer process, it could take more time than originally thought. Some issues may be resolved more quickly than you could imagine. The leader should err on the side of more time rather than not enough. Other team building, fellowship, worship, times of prayer, etc. can be employed if there is extra time and you are away from your work/ministry setting.

If discernment doesn't come during the time you have allotted, don't give up. Schedule another season of prayer whenever it works for the entire team. Encourage individuals to stay engaged with God on the journey until that time. Take time to talk with each team member to see how the process is unfolding. Find out where they may be struggling and where they are encouraged. Such debriefing will be invaluable. When you meet again, there should be some good insights and/or differences in the hearts and minds of those who have been pressing into God.

Seriously consider banning non-emergency cell phone usage during your process unless it is to connect with intercessors or spiritual advisors. No one is more important to talk with than God during this season of prayer. It is recommended that you use regular Bibles and journals rather than phones, iPads or laptops to avoid the temptation to check email, etc.

Step 6—Revisit Step 1:

Make sure everyone is fully aware and clear as to what the issue to be discerned or the decision to be made is.

Suggestions to Strengthen and Shape the Process

Spend time discussing these things with your team members:

Fasting is entirely appropriate in this process, and would be a good spiritual discipline to engage in as you travel this path. Perhaps choosing to skip at least one meal together to meet with God is a good start if fasting is not regularly practiced by team members. Be sensitive to people on the team who may not be able to fast for medical reasons and make this totally voluntary for all.

Worship continually. Worship is prayer, but not all prayer is worship. Spend significant amounts of time worshiping the Father at the beginning of your time together, as well as multiple times during the process as the Spirit leads. Worship will help your hearts step into the presence of God. It is not a human process you are engaging in but a supernatural one. Be sure to close out your season of prayer together with worship. If you are not comfortable leading out in worship, choose one or two others to be prepared to do so. You may find that worship begins to happen spontaneously throughout the journey you are taking.

Journal through the process. This is completely up to your team; however, it is strongly recommended that journaling be done both individually and corporately (perhaps via an appointed Scribe) so that you are able to see God move within and throughout this process. It will give you much valuable information and help you to see current and/or potential stumbling blocks as well as progress and unity of agreement. It will also give you an amazing look at how far you have come as a team and be a wonderful testimony to the working of God in your midst. More thankfulness will be generated in your hearts as you see your growth, and God's power, comfort, peace, presence, responses, etc. You will likely discover some things you didn't expect if you include the journaling component in your season of prayer together.

Spiritual Preparation:

As you prayerfully prepare your hearts, recognize that it is of much greater significance for your focus be upon your own character and the fruit that comes from Christ rather than the specific decisions or activities you engage in. Your relationship with Jesus is what will determine your life's direction and purposes. If you operate within His loving precepts, His will becomes clearer, because who you *are* is more important than what you *do* in the economy of God. If you want to emerge transformed and confident that you are operating within His will regarding His kingdom plans and purposes, you must align your hearts with His.

Each person on the decision-making/discernment team should individually spend time in prayer in the following areas prior to the retreat or gathering. Instruct team members to spend as much time as needed to work through these important heart issues. Photocopy and give each member the **Spiritual Preparation** worksheet on page 57-63. Challenge them to go through this process well ahead of the day you are to meet. Remind them once or twice before the event.

It would be very beneficial to journal through each one of these steps:

Confess Known Sin:

Take these scriptures deeply into your heart and meditate on them:

> "If I had not confessed the sin in my heart, the Lord would not have listened." *(Psalm 66:18 NLT)*

> "Search me, O God, and know my heart; test me and know my anxious thoughts. Point out anything in me that offends you, and lead me along the path of everlasting life." *(Psalm 139:23-24 NLT)*

> "Confess your sins to each other and pray for each other so that you may be healed. The earnest prayer of a righteous person has great power and produces wonderful results." *(James 5:16 NLT)*

Spend time examining your spiritual walk. Ask the Holy Spirit to search you. Then confess known sin. If He reveals something, confess it to God and possibly to another and repent of it (James 5:16). Be sure to receive the grace gift of forgiveness with gladness!

Is there a sin of omission that you need to confess to the Lord? James 4:17 says, "Therefore, to one who knows the right thing to do and does not do it, to him it is sin" (NASB).

Don't rush this time of confession, but allow the Holy Spirit to do a deep work in your heart. It shouldn't just be a recitation of sin, but a preparation for the transformative work God may want to do in and through you. It is important to know whether or not you are truly repentant for each of your wrongdoings and whether or not you are willing to relinquish them in favor of completely turning toward the holiness of Jesus.

Faith Check:

"It's impossible to please God apart from faith. And why? Because anyone who wants to approach God must believe both that he exists *and* that he cares enough to respond to those who seek him." *(Hebrews 11:6 MSG)*

Do you believe that God cares enough to respond to you personally and to your team corporately as you seek Him for discernment? If you have doubt in this area, why do you think that is? Ask God to meet you in this struggle and bring reassurance to your heart so that your faith is strengthened.

"But when you ask, you must believe and not doubt, because the one who doubts is like a wave of the sea, blown and tossed by the wind. That person should not expect to receive anything from the Lord. Such a person is double-minded and unstable in all they do." *(James 1:6-8 NIV)*

Is your faith strong enough to believe God for impossible and seemingly improbable things? Will you believe that God will give your team clarity and guide you to a decision or a point of discernment that reflects His perfect will? If you have difficulty in this area, perhaps your prayer should be, "I do believe, help me overcome my unbelief" (Mark 9:24 NIV)!

Some believe that God is going to do whatever God is going to do, no matter what we pray; however, Scripture clearly indicates the opposite. The Sovereign God, to a large extent, has limited the working of His power to the prayers of His people. Two examples in Scripture show us this: In Ezekiel 22:30, the Father looked for even one intercessor to stand before Him on behalf of the land, so that He wouldn't have to destroy it "but [He] found no one." Because an intercessor could not be found, the land was destroyed. In Exodus 32,

Moses interceded on behalf of the people and God reconsidered and relented from destroying them.

> "Be on guard. Stand firm in the faith. Be courageous. Be strong." *(1 Corinthians 16:13)*

Right Motives:

> "You ask and do not receive, because you ask with wrong motives, so that you may spend it on your pleasures." *(James 4:3 NASB)*

Prepare your heart to enter into a prayer covenant with your team with right motives rather than hidden intentions. Be sure that you will not be a hindrance or a stumbling block to others by going in to the discernment process trying to get your own way instead of seeking the way of God.

Forgiveness:

> "For if you forgive other people when they sin against you, your heavenly Father will also forgive you. But if you do not forgive others their sins, your Father will not forgive your sins." *(Matthew 6:14-15 NIV)*

Is there anyone in this leadership group or others whom you need to forgive or ask forgiveness from? Be sure to take care of this prior to the beginning of your discernment prayer time. Extending and receiving grace is crucial to building and maintaining relationships and unity.

> "Oh, what joy for those whose disobedience is forgiven, whose sins are put out of sight." *(Romans 4:7 NLT)*

Love One Another:

> "This is My commandment, that you love one another, just as I have loved you. Greater love has no one than this, that one lay down his life for his friends." (John 15:12-13 NASB)
> "So now I am giving you a new commandment: Love each other. Just as I have loved you, you should love each other. Your love for one another will prove to the world that you are my disciples." *(John 13:34-35 NLT)*
>
> "Be devoted to one another in love. Honor one another above yourselves." *(Romans 12:10 NIV)*

Can you truthfully say you love and honor each person with whom you are about to enter a season of prayer? Begin praying for anyone you struggle with relationally. Ask God to change your heart toward this person and give you His love for him or her.

Francis Frangipane in his book, *The Three Battlegrounds*, connects the importance of love with discernment: "Paul wrote, 'And this I pray, that your love may abound still more and more in real knowledge and all discernment' (Phil. 1:9). True discernment comes from abounding love. What is abounding love? It is love that leaps out from us toward others."

Ask God to move in such a way that what He shows you individually and collectively will be reflected in the love of Jesus flowing more freely from your lives into the lives of others.

7 Prayers for Discernment and Decision-Making

"Discernment can help you when you face decisions. Even though making good decisions can be difficult at times, trust that the Holy Spirit is with you to guide you and help you choose what is good and true.

"In essence, discernment is a decision-making process that honors the place of God's will in our lives. It is an interior search that seeks to align our own will with the will of God in order to learn what God is calling us to. Every choice we make, no matter how small, is an opportunity to align ourselves with God's will."

—Joe Paprocki, *Discernment: Making Inspired Choices*

After all of the preparatory work has been accomplished, initiate the **7 Prayers for Discernment and Decision-Making.**

Although they have been placed in a specific order, these prayers do not need to be prayed through as shown. Allow the Holy Spirit to guide you, interrupt you, change things up, etc.

In the beginning you may wish to walk through each of these prayers together just to familiarize your team with them. As already mentioned, you may find yourselves going back to one or several over and over again. Remember, this is a corporate prayer experience, but also an individual one. Allow the Father to show you which prayers to focus upon as you journey with Him. These seven prayers may not be the only components to employ. Take time to hear what the Spirit may be saying.

Something that may be very helpful in your process is to pray through the Scriptures listed with each prayer either individually or as a team. Suggested times for this are already indicated, but always remember to give the Holy Spirit room to alter the process.

You may wish to refer back to Specifics for the Process Leader #3-9 (Listed on pages 20-22) prior to this time to reflect and pray about how to shepherd your team through this process. For example, do you feel led to read most of the content and Scripture, or take turns with team members. I suggest that everything is read out loud in some way.

Don't be afraid of silence and don't be rushed. There should be no time schedule for this process as it should happen organically. When times of silence and solitude seem called for, the leader can make space for these things. Encourage individuals to change postures as they feel led. For example, if conviction comes one or more of the group might wish to kneel or lay face down on the floor. Be sensitive to the leading of the Holy Spirit, even if it means postponing progress.

Don't forget to stop, reflect, discuss, share and ask questions like, "Is anyone hearing from God?" Continually ask the Holy Spirit to be your guide as you move through these prayers together.

As long as there is unity of heart and agreement, the process can continue. If there is a roadblock or a sticking place, notify the intercessors to press in and take some time to be silent, asking the Father to help you break through into agreement (The Prayer of Unity).

> "Again I say to you, that if two of you agree on earth about anything that they may ask, it shall be done for them by My Father who is in heaven." *(Matthew 18:19 NASB)*

PRAYER OF INTERCESSION

"Christ teaches us to pray not only by example, instruction, command, and promises but also by showing us that He is our ever-living intercessor. When we believe this and abide in Him for our prayer life too, our fears of not being able to pray correctly will vanish. We will joyfully and triumphantly trust our Lord to teach us to pray and to be the life and power of our prayers. May God open our eyes to see what the glorious ministry of intercession is to which we as His royal priesthood have been set apart. May He help us to believe what mighty influence our prayers can have, and may all fear of being unable to fulfill our calling vanish as we grasp the truth that Jesus is living in us and interceding for us."

—Andrew Murray, *Teach Me to Pray*

> "It happened that while Jesus was praying in a certain place, after He had finished, one of His disciples said to Him, 'Lord, teach us to pray just as John also taught his disciples.'" *(Luke 11:1 NASB)*

Prayer is the one thing the disciples asked Jesus to teach them to do. Perhaps at the beginning of your prayer time together, you may wish to ask God to show you how to pray for His purposes and plans to be revealed as you seek to discern the way forward.

"The world is full of so-called prayer warriors who are prayer-ignorant. They're full of formulas and programs and advice, peddling techniques for getting what you want from God. Don't fall for that nonsense. This is your Father you are dealing with, and he knows better than you what you need. With a God like this loving you, you can pray very simply. Like this:" *(Matthew 6:7-8 MSG)*

"Our Father who is in heaven,
hallowed be Your name.
Your kingdom come.
Your will be done,
on earth as it is in heaven.
Give us this day our daily bread.
And forgive us our debts, as we also have forgiven our
    debtors.
And do not lead us into temptation, but deliver us from evil.
[For Yours is the kingdom and the power and the glory
forever. Amen."] *(Matthew 6:9-13 NASB)*

Individually: Ask God to make you a man or woman of prayer. Praying about your prayer life increases your awareness of your prayerlessness and will deepen your desire to build intimate relationship with the One who is on the other end of your prayer. Go after holiness through seeking His holiness.

"Draw near to God and He will draw near to you. Cleanse

your hands, you sinners; and purify your hearts, you dou-ble-minded." *(James 4:8 NASB)*

As a Team: Spend time laying out the decision that needs to be made, or the question/issue that needs to be discerned before God. Ask Him to receive it from your hands and take it into His heart. Pray for one another's hearts and lives. Ask God to knit you together into a cohesive team for the sake of His kingdom.

Affirm this together out loud: *"But seek first his kingdom and his righteousness, and all these things will be given to you as well" (Matthew 6:33 NIV).*

PRAYER OF LISTENING

"Discernment is the listening part of prayer: sitting with a question or decision in God's presence and waiting for the wisdom of God that is given as pure gift."

—Ruth Haley Barton, *Sacred Rhythms*

The prayer of listening should be engaged throughout the process to stay attentive to God's continual presence. It is also a way to become more fully aware of His peace and confirmation, as well as His comfort and strength whenever you don't know what to do or which step to take next. In an age of noise and distraction, it is difficult to be attuned to His voice alone, which is why it is such an important prayer practice.

Be sure to continually journal what God is saying both individually and corporately so that you are able to review how He is leading you. Not everything you hear needs to be directly related to the "issue" at hand. Sometimes it is just enough to spend time being still in His presence. Others have called this time "keeping company with God."

Spend a season being still and listening:

"Be still, and know that I am God; I will be exalted among the nations, I will be exalted in the earth!" *(Psalm 46:10 NIV)*

"Then the Lord came and stood and called as at other times, 'Samuel! Samuel' And Samuel said, 'Speak, for Your servant is listening.'" *(1 Samuel 3:10 NASB)*

"So Jesus said, 'When you have lifted up the Son of Man, then you will know that I am he and that I do nothing on my own but speak just what the Father has taught me. The one who sent me is with me; he has not left me alone, for I always do what pleases him.'" *(John 8:28-29 NIV)*

"I wait quietly before God,
   for my victory comes from him.
He alone is my rock and my salvation,
   my fortress where I will never be shaken."
(Psalm 62:1-2 NASB)

PRAYER OF THANKSGIVING

"Have the wisdom to perceive all there is to be thankful for, and then be thankful for the wisdom to perceive things so clearly."

—Richelle E. Goodrich, from *An Intimate Collision: Encounters with Life and Jesus,* by Craig D. Lounsbrough

Thankfulness is a posture of prayer that is often overlooked—especially in the midst of difficult or uncertain circumstances. As the discernment process takes shape, it is important to give thanks every step of the way. You may wish to come back to this place often as the Holy Spirit brings your hearts into alignment, and as progress toward clarity is made.

> "Be anxious for nothing, but in everything by prayer and supplication with thanksgiving let your requests be made known to God." *(Philippians 4:6 NASB)*

> "Let your roots grow down into him, and let your lives be built on him. Then your faith will grow strong in the truth you were taught, and you will overflow with thankfulness." *(Colossians 2:7 NLT)*

> "Let the peace of Christ rule in your hearts, to which indeed you were called in one body; and be thankful." *(Colossians 3:15 NASB)*

> "Since we are receiving a Kingdom that is unshakable, let us be thankful and please God by worshiping him with holy fear and awe." *(Hebrews 12:28 NLT)*

> "Devote yourselves to prayer, keeping alert in it with an attitude of thanksgiving." *(Colossians 4:2 NASB)*

You may wish to give thanks for what God has done in you individually and corporately. Break in continually to give thanks as you see Him moving you closer to His kingdom heart. Thank Him for answers, clarity, or anything else you may notice about the activity of God in your life and/or in your midst as a team.

PRAYER OF SUBMISSION

"In Gethsemane the holiest of all petitioners prayed three times that a certain cup might pass from Him. It did not."

—C.S. Lewis, "The Efficacy of Prayer" from *The World's Last Night and Other Essays*

The prayer of submission says, "Not my will but Yours be done." It is the prayer from the lips of Jesus that asks us to be indifferent to anything other than the perfect will of God.

> "And He withdrew from them about a stone's throw, and He knelt down and began to pray, saying, 'Father, if You are willing, remove this cup from Me; yet not My will, but Yours be done.'" *(Luke 22:41-42 NASB)*

It is the prayer that says, *"Your kingdom come. Your will be done, On earth as it is in heaven" (Matthew 6:10 NASB)*. So often, we prefer to come to God wanting our own will to be done in heaven as it is on earth.

In James 4:13-17, we are called to remember that we are just a "mist" or "vapor" in the grand scheme of God. We must be careful of an arrogance that makes this process all about us and our lives rather than all about God and His kingdom. It is critical to make sure that our thoughts and plans are aligned with His will and not our own. There is no option.

God is sovereign . . . and we are not! Seeking Him and His ways cannot be an after-thought as we look for answers and as we move forward. The future is only conditional upon God's will, not our own. Prayer cannot be left out of the process, for it is the way we communicate to and hear from God, Who alone knows what is on His heart for us!

God wants to put His personal spotlight on us as we focus on being inwardly thoughtful about what we are doing in our personal and corporate process of discernment. He will allow us to see where we are headed, but we must be willing to be introspective in order to make the appropriate course corrections and changes to align with His will, even when our own desires want so badly to break in.

> "See to it that no one takes you captive through philosophy and empty deception, according to the tradition of men, according to the elementary principles of the world, rather than according to Christ." *(Colossians 2:8 NASB)*

Just as Jesus submitted His will to the will of the Father, how much more should we do so? Pray through the passage of submission from Romans 12: 1-2 so that you may be more fully alive to the transformative purposes God has for you individually and corporately:

> "So here's what I want you to do, God helping you: Take your everyday, ordinary life—your sleeping, eating, going-to-work, and walking-around life—and place it before God as an offering. Embracing what God does for you is the best thing you can do for him. Don't become so well-adjusted to your culture that you fit into it without even thinking. Instead, fix your attention on God. You'll be changed from the inside out. Readily recognize what he wants from you, and quickly respond to it. Unlike the culture around you, always dragging you down to its level of immaturity, God brings the best out of you, develops well-formed maturity in you." *(Romans 12:1-2 MSG)*

The prayer of submission will likely take some significant time as deeply and firmly held personal desires, dreams or ideas are difficult to shake loose from so that they may be released into the care of God. You may even hear such things as, "I know what God's word says, but . . ." Or, "I think this is the only way that makes any sense . . ."

It could take returning to this place of prayer several times before every person on the team grasps the significance of dying to self and self's "great ideas" in this area.

> "We humans keep brainstorming options and plans, but God's purpose prevails." *(Proverbs 19:21 MSG)*

Pray with and for one another recognizing that submission is difficult.

PRAYER OF HUMILITY

"As long as you are proud you cannot know God. A proud man is always looking down on things and people: and, of course, as long as you are looking down you cannot see something that is above you."

—C.S. Lewis, "The Great Sin" from *Mere Christianity*

The prayer of humility requires great humility because it wrestles with letting go of the "my way is best" mentality. It releases anything that we have set up as an idol over something that God may wish to do.

This prayer puts leaders on the same page together, willing to hear from the Father for His plans and purposes.

Consider what baggage you might have brought in individually and collectively that could set itself up as an idol or multiple idols before God. Your idea or preconceived plans for this process could be the very things that slow the process down if you are unable to detach from them.

Perhaps the simplest prayer for individuals and/or the corporate team to pray would be:

"Lord, help me/us to release my/our grip on

_____ , which is keeping me/us from
moving forward toward aligning myself/ourselves with
Your plans and purposes for _____ .

Prayerfully consider these Scriptures individually and together:

"Next, learn to put aside your own desires so that you will become patient and godly, gladly letting God have his way with you." *(2 Peter 1:6 TLB)*

"He leads the humble in doing right, teaching them his way." *(Psalm 25:9 NLT)*

"The humble will see their God at work and be glad. Let all who seek God's help be encouraged." *(Psalm 69:32 NLT)*

"Whoever then humbles himself as this child, he is the greatest in the kingdom of heaven." *(Matthew 18:4 NASB)*

"For by the grace given me I say to every one of you: Do not think of yourself more highly than you ought, but rather think of yourself with sober judgment, in accordance with the faith God has distributed to each of you." *(Romans 12:3 NIV)*

"Be completely humble and gentle; be patient, bearing with one another in love." *(Ephesians 4:2 NIV)*

"Don't be selfish; don't try to impress others. Be humble, thinking of others as better than yourselves." *(Philippians 2:3 NLT)*

"He must become greater and greater, and I must become less and less." *(John 3:30 NLT)*

"So humble yourselves before God. Resist the devil, and he will flee from you." *(James 4:7 NLT)*

"Finally, all of you should be of one mind. Sympathize with each other. Love each other as brothers and sisters. Be tenderhearted, and keep a humble attitude." *(1 Peter 3:8 NLT)*

PRAYER OF WISDOM

"When the peace of God follows the purity of God's wisdom into our hearts and lives, it will affect those around us."

—David Jeremiah, *What to Do When You Don't Know What to Do*

"Some people go their entire lives without realizing that they are elevating their own wisdom and abilities above the Lord's."

—John Stange, "Overcoming Anxiety: 12 Powerful Truths"
from *Scripture for Defeating Worry and Fear*

The wisdom of this world is, as 1 Corinthians 3:19 teaches, foolishness to God. Yet, so often we seek our wisdom from worldly places rather than from the heart of God.

It is important to notice and acknowledge when answers are being sought first from places or people rather than the Father, even though other sources can certainly inform our decisions.

God is the place where true wisdom originates and perpetuates. His word has given us a very simple prayer for wisdom that has a promise attached to the answer if we will meet the condition—asking in faith:

"But if any of you lacks wisdom, let him ask of God, who

gives to all generously and without reproach, and it will be given to him. But he must ask in faith without any doubting, for the one who doubts is like the surf of the sea, driven and tossed by the wind. For that man ought not to expect that he will receive anything from the Lord, being a double-minded man, unstable in all his ways." *(James 1:5-8 NASB)*

Spend some time examining if there is any double-mindedness in your midst and ask God to give you all great faith to believe He will bring the wisdom you seek.

It is also important to glean insight from God's response to Solomon's prayer when he was given the opportunity to ask for anything he wanted:

"'So give your servant a discerning heart to govern your people and to distinguish between right and wrong. For who is able to govern this great people of yours?'

"The Lord was pleased that Solomon had asked for this. So God said to him, 'Since you have asked for this and not for long life or wealth for yourself, nor have asked for the death of your enemies but for discernment in administering justice, I will do what you have asked. I will give you a wise and discerning heart, so that there will never have been anyone like you, nor will there ever be.'" *(1 Kings 3:9-12 NIV)*

Solomon didn't ask for a wise and discerning *mind*, but a wise and discerning *heart*! If you are not careful, you can fall into the worldly trap of focusing only on your intellectual discernment that involves your ability to think, reason and grasp rather than inviting your mind to meet with your heart to discern your purposes, desires, hopes and dreams as they align with God's. As you can see in the passage, the Lord was pleased with Solomon's request and responded, *"I will do what you have asked. I will give you a wise and discerning heart" (v. 12).*

Use this passage as a reminder to focus on what God is doing with your hearts and not just your minds while you discern the way forward. You may wish to take some time to pray and discuss how this word from the Lord is important and why it may significantly impact your processing.

PRAYER OF UNITY

"If we are to enjoy the pleasures of unity we must use discernment constantly and consistently. We must put on the clothes of Christ's personality and character, chiefly humility and love, wisely choosing to pursue his course. Discern what words and behavior are most imitative of how Jesus would pursue engagement with others. Unity, oneness, with fellow believers is paramount in the eyes of God, and there is always a right path to discern how to get there and sustain it. You ought to choose to follow such a path of relationship, even if others around are not."

—James Montgomery, 1771-1854, from *Psalm 133*

Here is a time of critical importance. Leaders and decision-makers should be in complete unity about following the perfect will of the Father rather than staying attached to personal agendas or ideas. As long as the team stays unified, the way forward will have more clarity.

There may be times when people can "agree to disagree" about non-essential things and still move forward with unity. It is important that each person is able to freely express his or her opinions without fear of repercussion, humiliation or intimidation. Everyone's feelings should be valued and respected even when they are out of step with others. There may be underlying circumstances or reasons that need to be explored more fully.

As you pray for unity of heart, mind and purpose, the Holy Spirit will be at work to bring this about.

> "The glory which You have given Me I have given to them, that they may be one, just as We are one; I in them and You in Me, that they may be perfected in unity, so that the world may know that You sent Me, and loved them, even as You have loved Me." *(John 17:22-23 NASB)*

> "Behold, how good and how pleasant it is for brothers to dwell together in unity!" *(Psalm 133:1 NASB)*

> ". . . do not merely look out for your own personal interests, but also for the interests of others." *(Philippians 2:4 NASB)*

> "Therefore I, the prisoner of the Lord, implore you to walk in a manner worthy of the calling with which you have been called, with all humility and gentleness, with patience, showing tolerance for one another in love, being diligent to preserve the unity of the Spirit in the bond of peace." *(Ephesians 4:1-3 NASB)*

Dealing with Roadblocks

A potential roadblock may creep in here which will need to be addressed. If there is anyone on the leadership team who, after a reasonable amount of time, and after engaging in at least one season of prayer in all seven of the discernment prayers, is not able to move forward in unity of agreement, the process should be recessed, or individuals dismissed to seek the Lord on their own for a while.

The Leader should now take some time to meet with the person who is struggling to move into agreement. This is a good time for the Leader to engage intercessors using appropriate discretion. It is always possible that this one person may truly be hearing correctly from God, so it is crucial to be certain as to whether or not the rest of the group could be pursuing the wrong direction. God's rule is not majority rules. It is "His will be done!"

Be sure to have good confirmation from intercessors and other spiritual advisors before determining how to proceed from this point. If there is strong confirmation that the group is on the right track and if the person who is out of step with everyone else is not able or willing to re-engage the process with a desire to respond to the prayers of Submission and Humility particularly, or if there is some other issue that precludes moving forward with the team that cannot be resolved, he or she should lovingly be released from the process and therefore the decision or discernment at hand.

A second potential roadblock may trigger a need to revisit the **Preparation Prayers:** Confession, Faith, Obedience, Right Motives, Forgiveness, and Love.

It is important that no one feel they must capitulate or bend to the will of others, but only to the will of God. It is also important that no one harbors guilt or is struggling with the way the process is going. Periodically stop and put your finger on the pulse of your group. Urge your team to be completely honest if there are any problems, struggles, relationship issues, etc. so they may be dealt with.

Again, the Leader may wish to take time to talk with those who express concerns or issues by recessing the group for a time. If confession, forgiveness, etc. is needed, take the appropriate action as guided by the Holy Spirit. There should always be access to an outside advisor for those whose issue may be with the Leader.

"Our lives need to be responses from what God has given us, of indebtedness and love, so all we are and do is infused with His love and care, and so our decisions are made that way, too."

—Dr. Richard J. Krejcir, "Do Not Plan Ahead without God!" (Bible Study, James 4:13-17) © 2005 Dr. R.J. Krejcir, Into Thy Word Ministries www.intothyword.org

Moving Forward with Confidence

"Discernment is ongoing. After you make a decision, prayerfully evaluate it. If the fruits (outcomes) of your decision—your words, actions, and behaviors—are good, then it is a good indication that the decision you made is good. If the fruits are 'rotten,' then that is a good indication that you may need to alter your course. True discernment results in good fruit (even if it's something we wouldn't normally pick out for ourselves)."

—Joe Paprocki, *Discernment: Making Inspired Choices*

The goal for discerning God's will and for making the best possible decision is to move forward with confidence that you have heard from the Lord, gained clarity about your decision, and have a clear path for your next steps. To achieve this goal, you must ask some key questions:

1. What should we do if the clarity we seek hasn't come yet?

> "You say, 'But He has not answered.' He has, He is so near
> to you that His silence is the answer. His silence is big
> with terrific meaning that you cannot understand yet, but
> presently you will."
>
> —Oswald Chambers, *If You Will Ask: Reflections On the Power of Prayer*

Elijah wasn't sure what to do. He was being pursued by those who wished to kill him. He was discouraged and felt alone. He wasn't hearing clearly from the Lord about his next steps . . . and then:

> "'Go out and stand before me on the mountain,' the Lord told him. And as Elijah stood there, the Lord passed by, and a mighty windstorm hit the mountain. It was such a terrible blast that the rocks were torn loose, but the Lord was not in the wind. After the wind there was an earthquake, but the Lord was not in the earthquake. And after the earthquake there was a fire, but the Lord was not in the fire. And after the fire there was the sound of a gentle whisper. When Elijah heard it, he wrapped his face in his cloak and went out and stood at the entrance of the cave." *(1 Kings 19:11-13 NLT)*

It was at this point that God gave him his instructions. Elijah had obediently pursued the voice of God, and because he had relationship, he knew when he heard God speak. Elijah immediately obeyed the voice of God, and received encouragement to continue his ministry. Elijah had needed an encounter with the presence of God, and this encounter came in an unexpected whisper.

If, following your season of prayer, you feel God hasn't responded or given you the clarity you need, it is important to recognize that He may indeed have done just that but in a way you didn't expect or haven't yet perceived. Sometimes God seems very quiet. It is critical that you don't become discouraged, concerned or anxious. God's word is very clear about how we are to be at peace and not worried about anything. "Be anxious for nothing, but in everything by prayer and supplication with thanksgiving let your requests be made known to God" (Philippians 4:6 NASB).

Scripture has given us some very clear information about God's will: *"Rejoice always, pray continually, give thanks in all circumstances; for this is God's will for you in Christ Jesus" (1 Thessalonians 5:16-18 NIV).*

Give thanks to God for being present with you and for hearing your prayers. Believe that you have been heard and that God is at work, whether you perceive it or not. Recognize that His ways and thoughts are higher than yours: "For *as* the heavens are higher than the earth, so are My ways higher than your ways and My thoughts than your thoughts" (Isaiah 55:9 NASB).

If you do not receive confirmation, you will need to seek further clarity. Perhaps you rushed your process, or you need to once again examine your hearts through the **preparation prayers** and move through the **7 Prayers for Discernment and Decision-Making** again. Ask the Holy Spirit to guide you.

If you are confused or discouraged in any way by the process or the outcome, it would be a good idea to seek spiritual advisors to enter into the process of prayer with you in order to discern together the activity of God.

2. How can we be certain that our process is completed?

The best signal that you have reached an outcome aligned with the kingdom purposes of God is complete unity. Are you confident that you are all of one heart and mind and do you sense that God has guided you to the plan or decision that will bring Him the most honor and glory?

It may be that you already had God's plan from the beginning but just needed to be in one accord as a team. Or, an entirely new strategy, plan, direction or decision has emerged that had never been considered apart from seeking God. Regardless, at this point you will all know that you have the Father's confirmation and that moving forward together can now happen.

3. Do we need to seek outside confirmation if we are already confident we have heard from God?

When the end of your discernment time comes, it is the hope that, with the guidance of the Holy Spirit, you will have collectively heard from God in clarity and unity.

Sometimes, however, an important step in due diligence is to seek confirmation from two or more outside spiritual advisors. At this point it is likely that they will be able to validate your process; however, they might not. If so, prayerfully revisit together whatever concern has been raised.

When you have positive confirmation, you may feel confident that you have discerned and/or made a decision based on His word, is in His will, and that will allow for His kingdom purposes to be accomplished most fully and in great love.

Next Steps

If you have arrived at your decision with the sincere intention of pleasing the heart of God while incorporating biblical principles and wise counsel, you can proceed with confidence knowing that God will work out His purposes through your decision. It's time to act in obedience and accordance to what you have heard and received from God. He would not have revealed His will to you if He already knows you will not obey it. When you are completely submitted to God, His word will continue to be a lamp to your feet and a light to your path (Psalm 119:105). Consider the scriptures below:

"The person who trusts me will not only do what I'm doing but even greater things, because I, on my way to the Father, am giving you the same work to do that I've been doing. You can count on it. From now on, whatever you request along the lines of who I am and what I am doing, I'll do it. That's how the Father will be seen for who he is in the Son. I mean it. Whatever you request in this way, I'll do." *(John 14:12-14 MSG)*

"I am the Vine, you are the branches. When you're joined with me and I with you, the relation intimate and organic, the harvest is sure to be abundant. Separated, you can't produce a thing. Anyone who separates from me is deadwood, gathered up and thrown on the bonfire. But if you make yourselves at home with me and my words are at home in you, you can be sure that whatever you ask will be listened to and acted upon. This is how my Father shows who he is—when you produce grapes, when you mature as my disciples." *(John 15:5-8 MSG)*

"This is what I want you to do: Ask the Father for whatever is in keeping with the things I've revealed to you. Ask in my name, according to my will, and he'll most certainly give it to you. Your joy will be a river overflowing its banks!" *(John 16:23-24 MSG)*

"Trust in the Lord with all your heart; do not depend on your own understanding. Seek his will in all you do, and he will show you which path to take." *(Proverbs 3:5-6 NLT)*

"And we know that in all things God works for the good of those who love him, who have been called according to his purpose." *(Romans 8:28 NIV)*

"For everything created by God is good, and nothing is to be rejected if it is received with gratitude; for it is sanctified by means of the word of God and prayer." *(1 Timothy 4:4-5 NASB)*

Discernment—an Ongoing Process

Prayerfully evaluate as you step into the future, carefully making sure that the outcomes of your decision, as demonstrated in actions, words and behaviors, are bearing good fruit. It is important to continually appraise the decisions and plans made during your season of discernment prayer in case things change over time.

It is possible that what began to produce good, genuine fruit at one time, can deteriorate or change over time, especially if circumstances become different. Most importantly, don't slip back into old habits of going it alone apart from God. It is sometimes easy to get spiritually lazy and not shepherd the very purposeful plans of the Father that you spent time seeking after. *"We humans keep brainstorming options and plans, but God's purpose prevails" (Proverbs 19:21 MSG).*

If, at some point, you have a sense that God is urging you to alter your direction or plans, it may be time to enter into another season of prayer. The discernment process will become more natural as you find it easier to quickly move into alignment with God's heart. But it takes spiritual practice. As you step into God's plans and purposes each day, praying without ceasing will take on fresh meaning!

Extra Notes

If Churches are employing this guide as part of the **Roadmap to a Praying Church** partnership with Harvest Prayer Ministries, these resources are also recommended:

With One Accord in One Place: The Role of Prayer in the Early Church by Armin Gesswein

Forgotten Power: A Simple Theology for a Praying Church by David Butts

The Devil Goes to Church: Combatting the Everyday Attacks of Satan by David Butts

Participant's Guide

SPIRITUAL PREPARATION:

As you prayerfully prepare your hearts for the upcoming session or retreat, recognize that it is of much greater significance for your focus be upon your own character and the fruit that comes from Christ rather than the specific decisions or activities you engage in.

Your relationship with Jesus is what will determine your life's direction and purposes. If you operate within His loving precepts, His will becomes clearer, because who you *are* is more important than what you *do* in the economy of God. If you want to emerge transformed and confident that you are operating within His will regarding His kingdom plans and purposes, you must align your hearts with His.

As a member of the decision-making/discernment team please spend time in prayer in the following areas prior to the retreat or session. Spend as much time as you need to work through these important heart issues.

It would be very beneficial to journal through each one of these steps.

Confess Known Sin:

Take these scriptures deeply into your heart and meditate on them:

> "If I had not confessed the sin in my heart, the Lord would not have listened." *(Psalm 66:18 NLT)*

> "Search me, O God, and know my heart; test me and know my anxious thoughts. Point out anything in me that offends you, and lead me along the path of everlasting life." (Psalm *139:23-24 NLT)*

> "Confess your sins to each other and pray for each other so that you may be healed. The earnest prayer of a righteous person has great power and produces wonderful results." *(James 5:16 NLT)*

Spend time examining your spiritual walk. Ask the Holy Spirit to search you. Then confess known sin. If He reveals something, confess it to God and possibly to another and repent of it (James 5:16). Be sure to receive the grace gift of forgiveness with gladness!

Is there a sin of omission that you need to confess to the Lord? James 4:17 says, "Therefore, to one who knows the right thing to do and does not do it, to him it is sin" (NASB).

Don't rush this time of confession, but allow the Holy Spirit to do a deep work in your heart. It shouldn't just be a recitation of sin, but a preparation for the transformative work God may want to do in and through you. It is important to know whether or not you are truly repentant for each of your wrongdoings and whether or not you are willing to relinquish them in favor of completely turning toward the holiness of Jesus.

Notes from Confession Time:

_____

_____

_____

_____

_____

_____

_____

_____

Faith Check:

> "It's impossible to please God apart from faith. And why? Because anyone who wants to approach God must believe both that he exists _and_ that he cares enough to respond to those who seek him." _(Hebrews 11:6 MSG)_

Do you believe that God cares enough to respond to you personally and to your team corporately as you seek Him for discernment? If you have doubt in this area, why do you think that is? Ask God to meet you in this struggle and bring reassurance to your heart so that your faith is strengthened.

> "But when you ask, you must believe and not doubt, because the one who doubts is like a wave of the sea, blown and tossed by the wind. That person should not expect to receive anything from the Lord. Such a person is double-minded and unstable in all they do." _(James 1:6-8 NIV)_

Is your faith strong enough to believe God for impossible and seemingly improbable things? Will you believe that God will give your team clarity and guide you to a decision or a point of discernment that reflects His perfect will? If you have difficulty in this area, perhaps your prayer should be, "I do believe, help me overcome my unbelief" (Mark 9:24 NIV)!

Some believe that God is going to do whatever God is going to do, no matter what we pray; however, Scripture clearly indicates the opposite. The Sovereign God, to a large extent, has limited the working of His power to the prayers of His people.

Two examples in Scripture show us this: In Ezekiel 22:30, the Father looked for even one intercessor to stand before Him on behalf of the land, so that He wouldn't have to destroy it "but [He] found no one." Because an intercessor could not be found, the land was destroyed. In Exodus 32, Moses interceded on behalf of the people and God reconsidered and relented from destroying them.

> "Be on guard. Stand firm in the faith. Be courageous. Be strong." *(1 Corinthians 16:13)*

Notes from Faith Check:

_____

_____

_____

_____

_____

_____

Right Motives:

"You ask and do not receive, because you ask with wrong motives, so that you may spend *it* on your pleasures." *(James 4:3 NASB)*

Prepare your heart to enter into a prayer covenant with your team with right motives rather than hidden intentions. Be sure that you will not be a hindrance or a stumbling block to others by going in to the discernment process trying to get your own way instead of seeking the way of God.

Notes on Right Motives:

_____

_____

_____

_____

_____

_____

_____

_____

Forgiveness:

"For if you forgive other people when they sin against you, your heavenly Father will also forgive you. But if you do not forgive others their sins, your Father will not forgive your sins." *(Matthew 6:14-15 NIV)*

Is there anyone in this leadership group or others whom you need to forgive or ask forgiveness from? Be sure to take care of this prior to the beginning of your discernment prayer time. Extending and receiving grace is crucial to building and maintaining relationships and unity.

> "Oh, what joy for those whose disobedience is forgiven, whose sins are put out of sight." *(Romans 4:7 NLT)*

Notes on Forgiveness:

_____

_____

_____

_____

_____

_____

_____

_____

Love One Another:

> "This is My commandment, that you love one another, just as I have loved you. Greater love has no one than this, that one lay down his life for his friends." *(John 15:12-13 NASB)*

> "So now I am giving you a new commandment: Love each other. Just as I have loved you, you should love each other. Your love for one another will prove to the world that you are my disciples." *(John 13:34-35 NLT)*

"Be devoted to one another in love. Honor one another above yourselves." *(Romans 12:10 NIV)*

Can you truthfully say you love and honor each person with whom you are about to enter a season of prayer? Begin praying for anyone you struggle with relationally. Ask God to change your heart toward this person and give you His love for him or her.

Francis Frangipane in his book, *The Three Battlegrounds*, connects the importance of love with discernment: "Paul wrote, 'And this I pray, that your love may abound still more and more in real knowledge and all discernment' (Phil. 1:9). True discernment comes from abounding love. What is abounding love? It is love that leaps out from us toward others."

Ask God to move in such a way that what He shows you individually and collectively will be reflected in the love of Jesus flowing more freely from your lives into the lives of others.

Notes from Love One Another:

_____

_____

_____

_____

_____

_____

_____

_____

7 Prayers for Discernment and Decision-Making
(Participant's Guide)

PRAYER OF INTERCESSION

"It happened that while Jesus was praying in a certain place, after He had finished, one of His disciples said to Him, 'Lord, teach us to pray just as John also taught his disciples.'" (Luke 11:1 NASB)

Prayer is the one thing the disciples asked Jesus to teach them to do. Perhaps at the beginning of your prayer time together, you may wish to ask God to show you how to pray for His purposes and plans to be revealed as you seek to discern the way forward.

"The world is full of so-called prayer warriors who are prayer-ignorant. They're full of formulas and programs and advice, peddling techniques for getting what you want from God. Don't fall for that nonsense. This is your Father you are dealing with, and he knows better than you what you need. With a God like this loving you, you can pray very simply. Like this:" *(Matthew 6:7-8 MSG)*

"Our Father who is in heaven,
hallowed be Your name.
Your kingdom come.
Your will be done,
on earth as it is in heaven.
Give us this day our daily bread.
And forgive us our debts, as we also have forgiven our
    debtors.
And do not lead us into temptation, but deliver us from evil.
[For Yours is the kingdom and the power and the glory
forever. Amen."] *(Matthew 6:9-13 NASB)*

Individually: Ask God to make you a man or woman of prayer. Praying about your prayer life increases your awareness of your prayerlessness and will deepen your desire to build intimate relationship with the One who is on the other end of your prayer. Go after holiness through seeking His holiness.

"Draw near to God and He will draw near to you. Cleanse your hands, you sinners; and purify your hearts, you double-minded." *(James 4:8 NASB)*

As a Team: Spend time laying out the decision that needs to be made, or the question/issue that needs to be discerned before God. Ask Him to receive it from your hands and take it into His heart. Pray for one another's hearts and lives. Ask God to knit you together into a cohesive team for the sake of His kingdom.

Affirm this together out loud: *"But seek first his kingdom and his righteousness, and all these things will be given to you as well" (Matthew 6:33 NIV).*

Notes from Time of Intercession:

_____

_____

_____

_____

_____

_____

_____

_____

PRAYER OF LISTENING

The prayer of listening should be engaged throughout the process to stay attentive to God's continual presence. It is also a way to become more fully aware of His peace and confirmation, as well as His comfort and strength whenever you don't know what to do or which step to take next. In an age of noise and distraction, it is difficult to be attuned to His voice alone, which is why it is such an important prayer practice.

Be sure to continually journal what God is saying both individually and corporately so that you are able to review how He is leading you. Not everything you hear needs to be directly related to the "issue" at hand. Sometimes it is just enough to spend time being still in His presence. Others have called this time "keeping company with God."

Spend a season being still and listening:

> "Be still, and know that I am God; I will be exalted among the nations, I will be exalted in the earth!" _(Psalm 46:10 NIV)_

"Then the Lord came and stood and called as at other times, 'Samuel! Samuel' And Samuel said, 'Speak, for Your servant is listening.'" *(1 Samuel 3:10 NASB)*

"So Jesus said, 'When you have lifted up the Son of Man, then you will know that I am he and that I do nothing on my own but speak just what the Father has taught me. The one who sent me is with me; he has not left me alone, for I always do what pleases him.'" *(John 8:28-29 NIV)*

"I wait quietly before God,
    for my victory comes from him.
He alone is my rock and my salvation,
    my fortress where I will never be shaken."
(Psalm 62:1-2 NASB)

Notes from Time of Listening:

_____

_____

_____

_____

_____

_____

_____

_____

PRAYER OF THANKSGIVING

Thankfulness is a posture of prayer that is often overlooked—especially in the midst of difficult or uncertain circumstances.

Spend some time thanking God in prayer.

As the discernment process takes shape, it is important to give thanks every step of the way. You may wish to come back to this place often as the Holy Spirit brings your hearts into alignment, and as progress toward clarity is made.

> "Be anxious for nothing, but in everything by prayer and supplication with thanksgiving let your requests be made known to God." *(Philippians 4:6 NASB)*

> "Let your roots grow down into him, and let your lives be built on him. Then your faith will grow strong in the truth you were taught, and you will overflow with thankfulness." *(Colossians 2:7 NLT)*

> "Let the peace of Christ rule in your hearts, to which indeed you were called in one body; and be thankful." *(Colossians 3:15 NASB)*

> "Since we are receiving a Kingdom that is unshakable, let us be thankful and please God by worshiping him with holy fear and awe." *(Hebrews 12:28 NLT)*

> "Devote yourselves to prayer, keeping alert in it with an attitude of thanksgiving." *(Colossians 4:2 NASB)*

You may wish to give thanks for what God has done in you individually and corporately. Break in continually to give thanks as you see Him moving you closer to His kingdom heart. Thank Him for answers, clarity, or anything else you may notice about the activity of God in your life and/or in your midst as a team.

Notes from Time of Thanksgiving:

_____

_____

_____

_____

_____

_____

_____

_____

PRAYER OF SUBMISSION

The prayer of submission says, "Not my will but Yours be done." It is the prayer from the lips of Jesus that asks us to be indifferent to anything other than the perfect will of God.

Spend time submitting your will and agenda to His will.

> "And He withdrew from them about a stone's throw, and He knelt down and began to pray, saying, 'Father, if You are willing, remove this cup from Me; yet not My will, but Yours be done.'" (Luke 22:41-42 NASB)

It is the prayer that says, *"Your kingdom come. Your will be done, On earth as it is in heaven" (Matthew 6:10 NASB).* So often, we prefer to come to God wanting our own will to be done in heaven as it is on earth.

In James 4:13-17, we are called to remember that we are just a "mist" or "vapor" in the grand scheme of God. We must be careful of an arrogance that makes this process all about us and our agenda rather than all about God and His kingdom. It is critical to make sure that our thoughts and plans are aligned with His will and not our own. There is no option.

God wants to put His personal spotlight on us as we focus on being inwardly thoughtful about what we are doing in our personal and corporate process of discernment. He will allow us to see where we are headed, but we must be willing to be introspective in order to make the appropriate course corrections and changes to align with His will, even when our own desires want so badly to break in.

> "See to it that no one takes you captive through philosophy and empty deception, according to the tradition of men, according to the elementary principles of the world, rather than according to Christ." *(Colossians 2:8 NASB)*

Just as Jesus submitted His will to the will of the Father, how much more should we do so? Pray through the passage of submission from Romans 12:1-2 so that you may be more fully alive to the transformative purposes God has for you individually and corporately:

> "So here's what I want you to do, God helping you: Take your everyday, ordinary life—your sleeping, eating, going-to-work, and walking-around life—and place it before God as an offering. Embracing what God does for you is the best thing you can do for him. Don't become so well-adjusted to your culture that you fit into it without even thinking. Instead, fix your attention on God. You'll be changed from

the inside out. Readily recognize what he wants from you, and quickly respond to it. Unlike the culture around you, always dragging you down to its level of immaturity, God brings the best out of you, develops well-formed maturity in you." *(Romans 12:1-2 MSG)*

"We humans keep brainstorming options and plans, but God's purpose prevails." *(Proverbs 19:21 MSG)*

Pray with and for one another recognizing that submission is difficult.

Notes from Submission Time:

_____

_____

_____

_____

_____

_____

_____

_____

PRAYER OF HUMILITY

The prayer of humility requires great humility because it wrestles with letting go of the "my way is best" mentality. It releases anything that we have set up as an idol over something that God may wish to do.

This prayer puts leaders on the same page together, willing to hear from the Father for His plans and purposes.

Consider what baggage you might have brought in individually and collectively that could set itself up as an idol or multiple idols before God. Your idea or preconceived plans for this process could be the very things that slow the process down if you are unable to detach from them.

Perhaps the simplest prayer for you to pray would be:

"Lord, help me/us to release my/our grip on
_____, which is keeping me/us from moving forward toward aligning myself/ourselves with Your plans and purposes for _____.

Prayerfully consider these Scriptures individually and together:

"Next, learn to put aside your own desires so that you will become patient and godly, gladly letting God have his way with you." *(2 Peter 1:6 TLB)*

"He leads the humble in doing right, teaching them his way." *(Psalm 25:9 NLT)*

"The humble will see their God at work and be glad. Let all who seek God's help be encouraged." *(Psalm 69:32 NLT)*

"Whoever then humbles himself as this child, he is the greatest in the kingdom of heaven." *(Matthew 18:4 NASB)*

"For by the grace given me I say to every one of you: Do not think of yourself more highly than you ought, but rather think of yourself with sober judgment, in accordance with the faith God has distributed to each of you." *(Romans 12:3 NIV)*

"Be completely humble and gentle; be patient, bearing with one another in love." *(Ephesians 4:2 NIV)*

"Don't be selfish; don't try to impress others. Be humble, thinking of others as better than yourselves." *(Philippians 2:3 NLT)*

"He must become greater and greater, and I must become less and less." *(John 3:30 NLT)*

"So humble yourselves before God. Resist the devil, and he will flee from you." *(James 4:7 NLT)*

"Finally, all of you should be of one mind. Sympathize with each other. Love each other as brothers and sisters. Be tenderhearted, and keep a humble attitude." *(1 Peter 3:8 NLT)*

Notes from Prayer of Humility:

_____

_____

_____

_____

_____

_____

_____

_____

PRAYER OF WISDOM

The wisdom of this world is, as 1 Corinthians 3:19 teaches, foolishness to God. Yet, so often we seek our wisdom from worldly places rather than from the heart of God.

God is the place where true wisdom originates and perpetuates. His word has given us a very simple prayer for wisdom that has a promise attached to the answer if we will meet the condition—asking in faith:

> "But if any of you lacks wisdom, let him ask of God, who gives to all generously and without reproach, and it will be given to him. But he must ask in faith without any doubting, for the one who doubts is like the surf of the sea, driven and tossed by the wind. For that man ought not to expect that he will receive anything from the Lord, being a double-minded man, unstable in all his ways." *(James 1:5-8 NASB)*

Spend some time examining if there is any double-mindedness in you midst and ask God to give you all great faith to believe He will bring the wisdom you seek.

It is also important to glean insight from God's response to Solomon's prayer when he was given the opportunity to ask for anything he wanted:

> "'So give your servant a discerning heart to govern your people and to distinguish between right and wrong. For who is able to govern this great people of yours?'
>
> "The Lord was pleased that Solomon had asked for this. So God said to him, 'Since you have asked for this and not for long life or wealth for yourself, nor have asked for the death of your enemies but for discernment in administering justice, I will do what you have asked. I will give you a wise and discerning heart, so that there will never have been

anyone like you, nor will there ever be.'" *(1 Kings 3:9-12 NIV)*

Solomon didn't ask for a wise and discerning *mind*, but a wise and discerning *heart*! If you are not careful, you can fall into the worldly trap of focusing only on your intellectual discernment that involves your ability to think, reason and grasp rather than inviting your mind to meet with your heart to discern your purposes, desires, hopes and dreams as they align with God's. As you can see in the passage, the Lord was pleased with Solomon's request and responded, *"I will do what you have asked. I will give you a wise and discerning heart"* (v. 12).

Notes from Prayer of Wisdom:

_____

_____

_____

_____

_____

_____

PRAYER OF UNITY

Here is a time of critical importance. Leaders and decision-makers should be in complete unity about following the perfect will of the Father rather than staying attached to personal agendas or ideas. As long as the team stays unified, the way forward will have more clarity.

As you pray for unity of heart, mind and purpose, the Holy Spirit will be at work to bring this about.

"The glory which You have given Me I have given to them, that they may be one, just as We are one; I in them and You in Me, that they may be perfected in unity, so that the world may know that You sent Me, and loved them, even as You have loved Me." *(John 17:22-23 NASB)*

"Behold, how good and how pleasant it is for brothers to dwell together in unity!" *(Psalm 133:1 NASB)*

". . . do not merely look out for your own personal interests, but also for the interests of others." *(Philippians 2:4 NASB)*

"Therefore I, the prisoner of the Lord, implore you to walk in a manner worthy of the calling with which you have been called, with all humility and gentleness, with patience, showing tolerance for one another in love, being diligent to preserve the unity of the Spirit in the bond of peace." *(Ephesians 4:1-3 NASB)*

Notes from Prayer of Unity:

_____

_____

_____

_____

_____

_____

_____

Do you want to see a greater passion for prayer in your church?

Are you equipped to be a catalyst for prayer in your congregation?

Then you need to be a member of the

The Church Prayer Leaders Network exists to encourage, challenge, inspire, and resource you as you seek to motivate and mobilize your church toward deeper levels of prayer.

Benefits of Membership:
- Annual subscription to *Prayer Connect* magazine
- Receive "Prayer Leader Online," a bi-monthly email that includes suggestions, inspiration and resource ideas to help you in your ministry of developing prayer.
- Discounts on prayer resources at prayershop.org

Go to prayerleader.com/membership or call 812 238-5504 to join.

PRAYERCONNECT

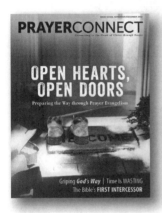  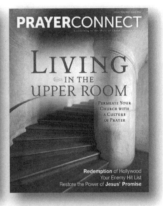

A QUARTERLY MAGAZINE DESIGNED TO:

Mobilize believers to pray God's purposes for
their church, city and nation.

Connect intercessors with the growing worldwide prayer movement.

Equip prayer leaders and pastors with tools
to disciple their congregations.

Each issue of *Prayer Connect* includes:
- Practical articles to equip and inspire your prayer life.
- Helpful prayer tips and proven ideas.
- News of prayer movements around the world.
- Theme articles exploring important prayer topics.
- Connections to prayer resources available online.

Print subscription: $24.99
(includes digital version)

Digital subscription: $19.99

Church Prayer Leaders Network membership: $35.99 (includes print, digital, and CPLN membership benefits)

SUBSCRIBE NOW.
www.prayerleader.com/membership or call 800-217-5200

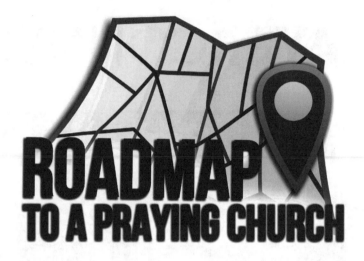

ROADMAP
TO A PRAYING CHURCH

Develop a roadmap to guide your church
----------- on a journey to become -----------
a House of Prayer for all Nations!

Let Harvest Prayer Ministries come alongside your leadership team to help you discern and strategize how you can grow the prayer level of your church and develop disciples who impact the kingdom of God in significant ways.

For more information:
harvestprayer.com or 812 230-3130

HARVEST PRAYER
MINISTRIES